PIANO • VOCAL • GUITAR

THE BEST OF GILBERT O'SULLIVAN

ISBN 978-1-61774-119-7

HAL•LEONARD® CORPORATION

7777 W. BLUEMOUND RD. P.O. BOX 13819 MILWAUKEE, WI 53213

Photo Courtesy of Grand Upright Music

Visit Hal Leonard Online at
www.halleonard.com

GILBERT: AN APPRECIATION

by Michael Feeney Callan

I have a clear remembrance of the first (and hopefully last) time I offended Gilbert O'Sullivan. We were discussing his song writing and I misremembered a title (the song was *We Will*) and I saw the fleeting look of anguish in his face. It told me two things: that unconsciously I viewed his songs not in the singular but as a long, organic stream of work–like, say, Walt Whitman's famous lifelong poem *Leaves of Grass*–and, more importantly, in terms of understanding the artist, that Gilbert's devotion to his songs was paternal and individual, that he crafted every single one with love and cherished it.

Misinterpreting Gilbert O'Sullivan's work has been, from time to time, a national pastime. In 2006 he released one of his most potent records in years, *A Scruff at Heart*. Its curatorial root–a signature interest in childhood, growth and social awareness that saturates all his work–was as strong as ever. But it came in a self-designed CD box that highlighted a controversial socio-political statement about equalizing the rights of Palestinians with the ambitions of Israelis. Briefly, all hell broke loose, though Gilbert's humanitarian stance has been consistent since as far back as 1971's *Nothing Rhymed* where he implored us all to think twice about moral duties to the poor as we ate "more than enough apple pie." The great tragedy about such sensationalized over-reaction is the fact that it overshadowed the accomplishments of a triumphant work: songs like *Take Your Foot Off My Toe*, with a stunning sliding chord backing track that George Martin in his heyday would have been proud of (Gilbert self-produced), and the ingenious wordplay of *Just So You Know* that would have made Cole Porter green with envy.

An apparent hot potato issue with Gilbert (or Ray, as he is known to kith and kin) is the descriptive monicker so often appended to his name: "singer-songwriter," a connotation, in the pop world, that suggests Billy Joel or Elton John. On 1997's *Singer Sowing Machine*, the first album recorded at his now-in-daily-use purpose-built home studio in Jersey, he wryly mocked the phrase, revealing a resistance to imposed labels that underscores his fundamental obsession with originality and honesty. In the media, too easily it seems, Gilbert O'Sullivan is marked as contentious and rebellious because he wrestled for more than a decade with former manager Gordon Mills for equitable royalties and the restoration of his copyrights and, later, upended industry apathy by challenging a rap artist who "sampled" (read, "stole") one of his songs. But the declaration of unshakeable independence–and being just plain different–was there from the start.

Gilbert was twenty-one when he wrote *I Wish I Could Cry* in response to the assassination of the "Great Youth Hope," Robert Kennedy. His recording was thwarted by the corporate maestros of a now-forgotten record label who sought to prettify it, but at least he managed to force this and two other template songs that would signal his career, *Disappear* and *Mr Moody's Garden*, into the light of day. What became clear, three full years before his first album suite, *Himself*, emerged, was his originality. All three songs, lyrically and in their texturally varied vocal approach, are not relatable to anything that was happening in rock or pop at that time. To find their closest relation we'd go back more than fifty years to the Yale drama society of 1912, where an ambitious student, Cole Porter, emerged with *And the Villain Still Pursued Her*, a spoof of *Uncle Tom's Cabin*:

> I take delight
> In looking for a fight
> And pressing little babies on the head.... *

Seemingly effortlessly, Gilbert could match him:

> Houdini said to get out of bed
> Was the hardest thing he could do
> Yet when he's tied, strait-jacket plied
> He's out at the count of two ... *

The contortionist lyrics, though, were less than the half of it. Gilbert had something to say, musically and otherwise. A piano composer, as opposed to the burgeoning pop-rock trend of guitar composition, his melodies had the vertical shape that the late musicologist Ian MacDonald ascribed to McCartney's song writing (in contrast to Lennon's "horizontal" composition). To be sure, his closest style rival was always McCartney who, like Gilbert, frequently married music hall sensibilities to acerbic commentary. The pop-rock boys drew from the well of jazz and blues. But sonically, like McCartney, Gilbert embraced the entire musical landscape of what had gone before, without bias. He could rough-rock with the best of them on *Get Down*, his third million-selling single, but you were likely to receive a quasi-homily like *Where Peaceful Waters Flow* or a piano-only (with dabs of orchestra) album like 1994's *By Larry* by way of follow up.

Like McCartney, the central concept of "home", redemption and hope define Gilbert's oeuvre. His songs fall into three categories: songs of social observation (even agitation), humor and romance. The barbs reward the careful listener, and are as acute as many a protest poet at full flight. Disillusioned by the busted flush of the hippies and all that sixties' youth culture entrained, Gilbert had lots to say. On *Himself*, he lambasted social ennui in *Permissive Twit*; elsewhere he hit out at a lax media (*Too Much Attention*, from *Himself*), pervasive violence (*What's It All Supposed to Mean*, from *Pianoforeplay*) and bullying (*Don't Let It Get to You*, from *A Scruff at Heart*). These observations are as blisteringly direct as his Palestinian commentary on the *Scruff* sleeve work, but they are always leavened by deepest, passionate feeling. *Lost a Friend*, from *In the Key of G*, is far and away the most moving song about the assassination of John Lennon ever written. Gilbert's global viewpoint is also, of course, elevated by roll-on-the-floor humor. Humor, those close to him will tell you, is his lodestar, and one suspects it is also a sanity preserve. Who has heard *Disappear* (from *Caricature*, the 2003 Rhino box set), his half-serious mission statement, and not smiled? Who hasn't heard Edward Lear's bible of absurdities in *Ooh-Wakka-Do-Wakka-Day*?

And then, of course, there are the romances. Cumulatively, they are Gilbert's greatest achievement. In the same encyclopaedic fashion as his use of old music forms, they cover the prism, from pulverizing heartbreak in *Alone Again (Naturally)*, to the exquisite simplicity of romantic rightness in *The Niceness of It All*. Writing a love song, Carl Wilson of the Beach Boys once told me, is the hardest challenge of all. The great French poet Mallarme believed in the power of allusion. And in the best love songs of Porter, of Irving Berlin, or Jerome Kern, it is less the specifics and more the mood that delivers the feeling. Gilbert is a past master at mood-making. Listen again to 1973's *Why, Oh Why, Oh Why* or 2006's *My Place or Yours* to remind yourself of the galactic gravity of that best thing we will ever know: true love.

In the overview of his marathon, untiring career, it's clear that stubborn independence and broad ambition equally define Gilbert O'Sullivan. We should be grateful for both attributes. In his Charlie Chaplinesque beginnings–resisted by his management–he gave notice of the intransigence to come. "The business" is the bane of all artists' lives. One of the greatest nineteenth century novelists, Herman Melville, had his career effectively stopped by the bad critiques of *Moby Dick*; he never wrote again and remained silent for thirty years till his death. On his grave in Woodlawn Cemetery in New York he requested a blank page be carved in stone, symbolizing his loss.

But Gilbert O'Sullivan prevails. He continues to labor daily at his studio in Jersey, continues to mirror the world and all its peccadilloes, continues to love love. Already he is at work on the new album. There will be no blank pages for Gilbert.

Michael Feeney Callan has a new biography of Robert Redford published by Knopf, New York.

CONTENTS

CLAIR

Words and Music by
GILBERT O'SULLIVAN

Clair, _____ the mo-ment I met _____ you, I swear, _____ I felt as if some-thing some-where _____ had hap-pened to me, _____ which I could-n't see. _____ And

ALL THEY WANTED TO SAY

Words and Music by
GILBERT O'SULLIVAN

ALONE AGAIN NATURALLY

Words and Music by
GILBERT O'SULLIVAN

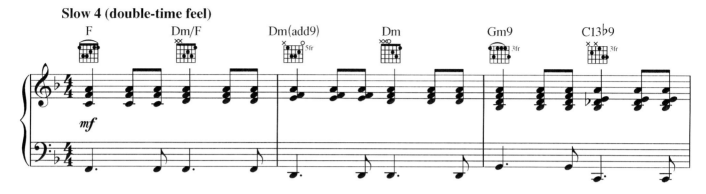

Slow 4 (double-time feel)

Oh, in a lit-tle while from now, __ if I'm
___ that on-ly yes-ter-day, __ I was
look-ing back o-ver the years, and

not feel-ing an-y less so-ur, I prom-ise my-self to treat__ my-self and vis-
cheer-ful bright and gay; look-ing for-ward to, well, who would-n't do the role__
what-ev-er else that ap-pears, I re-mem-ber I cried when my fa-ther died, nev-er

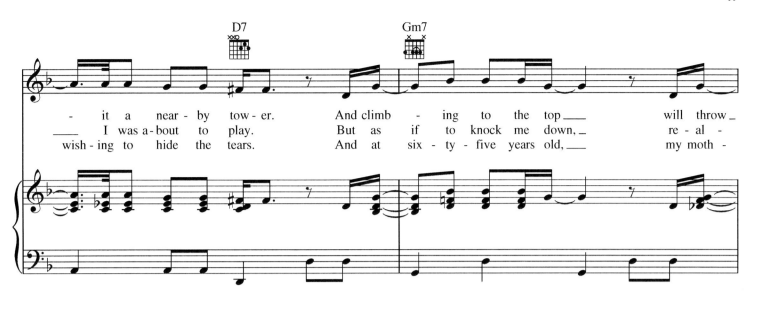

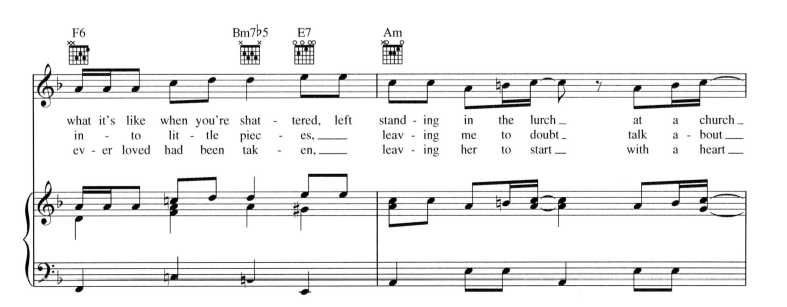

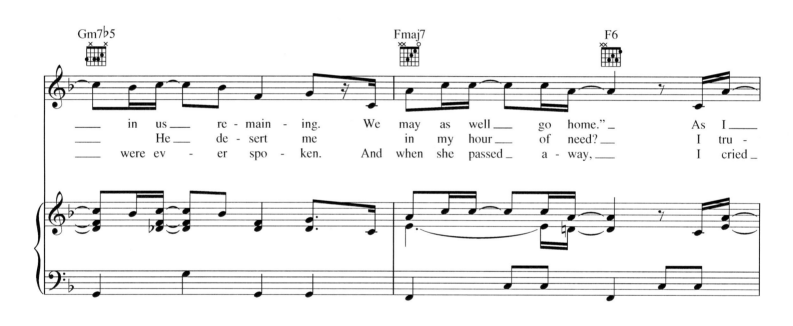

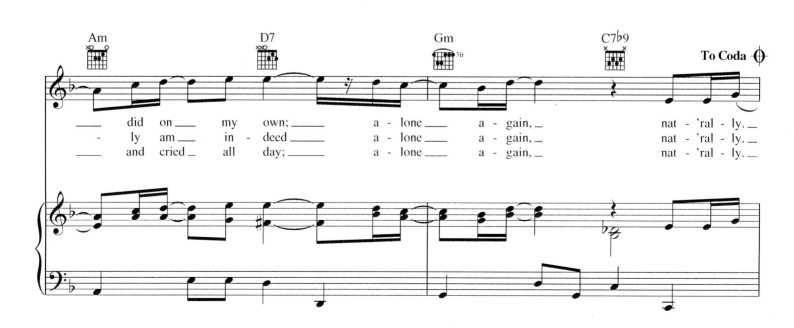

CAN'T THINK STRAIGHT

Words and Music by
GILBERT O'SULLIVAN

(Spoken:) "Hello?" "Oh, is, ah, Mary there?" "No." "Well..."

If you see Mar-y, will you tell her I called? Tell her that I love her and I'm sor-ry, that's all. You

GET DOWN

Words and Music by
GILBERT O'SULLIVAN

MISSING YOU ALREADY

Words and Music by
GILBERT O'SULLIVAN

MATRIMONY

Words and Music by
GILBERT O'SULLIVAN

It's mat - ri - mo - ny. _____

That's mat - ri - mo - ny. _____

Oh, I'm tru - ly grate - ful for ___ the lit - tle things in life ___ that have

NOTHING RHYMED

Words and Music by
GILBERT O'SULLIVAN

OUT OF THE QUESTION

Words and Music by
GILBERT O'SULLIVAN

Slowly

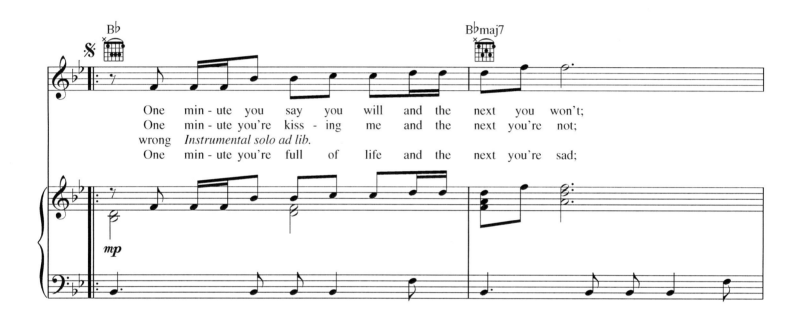

One min - ute you say you will and the next you won't;
One min - ute you're kiss - ing me and the next you're not;
wrong *Instrumental solo ad lib.*
One min - ute you're full of life and the next you're sad;

one min - ute you want ___ me ___ and the next ___ you don't.
one min - ute you re - mem - ber ___ and the next ___ you've for - got.

one min - ute you're mar - vel - ous and the next ___ you're bad.

WE WILL

Words and Music by
GILBERT O'SULLIVAN

WHAT'S IN A KISS

Words and Music by
GILBERT O'SULLIVAN

NO MATTER HOW I TRY

Words and Music by
GILBERT O'SULLIVAN